The Book Of Muh, The Not Funny Joke Book

Written by Michael Alcaraz

Why I Wrote This Book

I'm the type of guy who keeps entertained in the head easily and walks 12 miles a day. I went to Open Mics, but realized they are very time consuming for a 3 to 7-minute set. There are a bunch of politics and I was not about to play buddy-buddy. I sure wowed the crowd most nights. I got offers to play at big shows, but it's hard to bring 12 people and have them spend $40. Therefore, I wrote this book to have a one on one comedy performance with each reader/ fan. My grammar might be a little off, but I can think of an idea. I would also like to thank my one friend; you know who you are. This is not your typical comedy book. I'm just a scrappy kid from Irvine California chained to a fence and swinging. Enjoy!

-Michael Alcaraz

P.S. I love you Mom, Grandma, Dad, Jon, Nick, Sara, Dee, Tio, Son, and Skip.

There was no Braille to touch, so I read.

Copyright © 2017 by Michael Alcaraz

What's a boxer's favorite type of fish? Sockeye Salmon.

What's a bodybuilder's favorite food? Mussels.

I'm not calling you a baby, but the only thing I hear coming from your mouth is goo-goo-ga-ga-goo.

"What's your number?" "My number is 9-1-1."

"Where did my shoes go?" "I heard they walked off."

"I tried to move a rock, but it was not moving. . . . kind of like my life." – Mr. Kim

My dog is fashionable. What magazine highlights fashionable dogs? Doggy Style Magazine.

What do cool athletes drink? Kool Aid.

What type of healthcare do most Christians have? Blue Cross.

My favorite ride at Disneyland used to be the Matterhorn because the girl could sit in my lap and make me mad-a-horny.

If a guy wants to see if a girl likes him, he should ask to see if she's interested in taking him to the Sadie Hawkins Dance.

So unpopular these days, can't even buy a like on social media.

Been rejected so many times that my list is longer than Santa's Naughty List.

What's a serial killer's favorite type of breakfast? Cereal.

Where does all the money in the wishing wells go? Wells Fargo.

What do the Chinese eat their food off? China.

Why did the officer have trouble getting leads for crimes? Because snitches get stitches.

Mom said things were a little tight this holiday season. With Christmas around the corner I'm trying to recall if she said I was getting clothes, coal, or something from Kohls.

What is the most popular food to eat in May? Mayonnaise.

If Magic Johnson was a magician and Larry Bird was an animal, what would the magician pull out of a hat? A bird.

The airport metal detector kept going off. Told TSA "It must be my arms from lifting so much iron."

Marketing slogan for Subway. "Eat Subway and you will be hungry in two hours. See you soon."

What is the backup football player's position called? Left Out.

Name a queer fraternity? Alpha Faggot Omega.

Why was the teacher kicked out of the teacher supply store? Because he asked the clerk if they sold whips for naughty children.

Bueno Mars the musician.

Balby Dawn, Bruce Molina, Hammy Duke, Jim Wise, Pucky the Grinch, and Adeldo Chavez all ate ham and cheese sandwiches.

What did the fast food worker give to the attractive customer? Hot sauce.

In rural America the town idiot went on a walk. After a few miles, he suddenly stopped. Why? Because he arrived at a "STOP" sign.

Mirror, mirror on the wall who's the smoothest of them all? A shaved man.

What do you call a husband and wife having an argument on the soap aisle at the grocery store? A soap opera.

If the Bloods like Bloody Mary's, what do the Crips like? Crapes.

If The Groundhog indicates the end of Winter and the start of Spring, what creature indicates the start of Summer? A June Bug.

Who is the Ultimate Hipster? The one who can hula-hoop the longest.

What kind of music does a rat listen to? Trap.

What is the worst way to get arrested at a fast food restaurant? Getting caught putting soda in a water cup when a cop is behind you.

Besides the person with alcohol at the party, who is the second coolest person in attendance? The person who brings the chips or is it the person who calls the cops?

The Lakers are doing good this year. Do you think Shak and Colby have what it takes to win another championship?

Recently watched Titanic. Jack and Rose should win the ESPY for Best Team!

A girl can cause a lot of horror if she gives a guy a STD. What a whore!

When walking your dog on a cold night, picking up your dog's poop with your hand is a nice way to keep warm.

While at a retail store, the product would not scan at the checkout. The customer said "It's free." The clerk said "And I'm free to shove my fist down your throat."

"They're either thanking me or they're spanking me," said the stripper.

Why do go-go dancers drink a lot of milk shakes? So they can shake better.

Statistics say people seek members of their race. Will Snow White seek a Snow Man?

Why did everyone pull out their phone to record the song at the concert? To miss out on the moment.

"Sir I'm going to have to call security if you don't leave." "Just call the cops."

It's kind of a scary time to be alive right now so beware of terrorist propaganda such as ISIS Crème, a dessert to die for.

How did the teenager pay for his pet duck? With a bill.

How bad was the man's penmanship? So bad that he told people he wrote in code to protect the authenticity of his ideas.

He texted her ten hours ago. No response. He texted her five hours later. No response. Did her phone break? Or does he need to take his phone back to Verizon?

Hand sanitizer claims to kill the most germs. Did a Jewish person invent hand sanitizer?

What shoe is most talked about? A lot of people wear Converse shoes. Now that is something to converse about.

Traffic. You want to talk about traffic? It can be a real pain in the asphalt.

"I'm going to beat you up freshman kid." "Can I just stuff myself in a trashcan so we can go about our days?"

"Got any assets?" "Yeah, two movie tickets that are already paid for."

Ef eye knew howell 2 spall eye kood be eh poit.

"Send this man to the Looney Bin, he is absolutely crazy." "If I'm that crazy, send me to the Looney Bin-Laden."

Every day in America is spooky; therefore, Halloween is year-round.

"Who let the dogs out?" "Put on your shoes."

Pick Up line. "Excuse me, is this where our love story begins? If no one tells you that you are beautiful, know that you are beautiful. Now let me bask in your splendor."

Online dating platform said DoGsaidWOOF90 and Cutie BabyXD have a 0 percent match. DoGsaidWOOF90: "0% match, I'll take my chances. We can have a feast using my EBT government food stamps."

I was a Broncos fan before Peyton Manning, before Tim Tebow, and before John Elway. I became a Broncos fan because of OJ. . . . and his white bronco.

"Endless apps at Fridays? Great, I'll take an Angry Birds." – Ethan Chandler

What did the New York stockbrokers listen to after a lucrative trading day? Green Day.

A crop farmer came out of his barn and smelled a strong stench. "Oh what could it be he wondered?" He saw no animal carcasses and had sprayed no pesticides. His crop partner turned to him and said "Sorry, I crop-dusted" and laughed. The farmer then went "PEEEEYEEEEEW."

"What's your favorite EDM song?" "The one that goes beep, bop, beep, beep, bass, bass, bop beep."

3 + 7 = 12   5 x 1 = 6.5   9 – 4 = 13

Add the sums. 12 + 6.51 + 13 = 31.51

"You get an F."

"Sorry my peanut size brain is having technical difficulties."

A server will get a 20% tip if he or she acknowledges the loaf of bread on my head.

It's not what your dogs can do for you; it's what you can do for your dogs.

How does a poor man get an acupuncture? He jumps into a cactus.

SET LIST FOR THE SOLD-OUT CONCERT

- Filling My Time Up In The Shade
- No Search Party
- The Text Message That Never Came
- Never Had Girl Problems
- Friends Aren't For Me
- Goonies Taking Out The Trash
- Tall Glass Of Bleach For Happy Hour
- Crying On Halloween
- Life With No Love
- She For A Second
- Grinch In A Cadillac

"You guys have been great!" "One more song. One more song!" the crowd cheers. "You guys want to hear a song we're not releasing till next month?" The crowd goes bonkers. "This next one is going to be a real classic and you're hearing it for the very first time. This one is called *Table For One!*" The stands erupt in pandemonium.

OH YOU WANT MORE? TIME TO SPICE IT UP A BIT. Zesty, crunchy, soft, moist, refreshing, cool, yummy, bueno, spicy meatball.

Why did the guy want to go to Texas? To say, "I'm a Big Texas Queer."

What must go on a sandwich? Mustard.

When the man went to snitch on his co-worker, what was the first thing out of his mouth to his boss? "When you're not here, I like to be your set of eyes."

Does anyone's cheeks hurt? Well if they do, look at me like I'm an EMT. If you need anything, I'll be right there!

"What do you think of the show so far?" "It's good, but it would be great if I had some popcorn and earplugs. Your jokes suck!"

The future of comedy is on the line. **Best Comedy Book of 2017.** Humor 20 years before it's time. Is he out of his mind or is he a genius? Grandfather humor. *The pages turn themselves.* Funniest comedy book since Jokes for Kids 2002. Comedy Day's of Our Lives. The comedy world has stopped to glance. THE GREAT COMEDY STRIKE IS OVER: WORKER BEES RESUME WORK. The kids are talking about this type of comedy at the drinking fountains. A comedy discussion that will carry on through the years. Mike the Beatnik.

Everything's so expensive these days. I recently had to start saving my fast food cups. A Hardee's cup of mine made it to four different locations last week.

I was looking to start a new hobby and get into scuba diving, but that can be kind of expensive. To offset the cost I was thinking I could go scuba diving in public fountains and start collecting coins.

A sweaty man (Mr. Styles) with sun baked skin walks in to the establishment. "I'll take a number 7." "Sir I cannot serve you." The lady points to the sign. A few minutes later the man comes back wearing a toilet seat safe guard cover and says "I'll take a number 7. I want a large Dr. Pepper and curly fries. Oh and my shirt is designer." "Get a real shirt. The 99 Cent Store is next door."

Knock-knock?

Who's there?

Mr. Dog.

Mr. Dog who?

Woof.

"Times are tough. I went from pennies to pocket lint." – Ethan Chandler

L G B T Q. . . .X Y Z. . . .now I know my ABC's.

Popular Restaurants:
Fairy Queen Ice Cream
Pucky Cheese, a place for kids to play.

Herman: You on Facebook?
Andold: No, never was one for friends.

Santa: Young boy, what do you want for Christmas?

Charlie: I want a ball and chain shackle, coal, and a pack of cigarettes for mother who is currently pregnant.

Yesterday I was glued to the TV all day. The only name I responded to was Elmer.

Dollnald Trump, Dawnald Dump, Dollson's Creek, Dolly Parker, Doll Train.

"Everything was going fine, but then the guy called me a "little homie gay a*s, no good b*#!h a*s trick a**, snitch a*s, mother fu$#er witch a** grinch, venomous snake b*#ch!"'

So I've been trying to grow my network on LinkedIn in microbiology, business, and mathematics. No one is endorsing me. So I sent request to get endorsed as a panzy and everyone is endorsing me.

I'm fortunate enough to have all my teeth, but if I only had 3 teeth. . . .I sure would spend a lot of time brushing them each day.

"Loving this coffee mhmm."
"What can I send to the kitchen for ya sweetheart?"
" A Grand Islam?"
"Excuse me?"
"A Grand Slam?"
"Bacon or sausage?"
"Sausage."
"Everyone else has ordered bacon this morning."
"Everyone else is also ugly."
"I love bacon."
"Cancel my order."
"Why?"
"Leave me alone. Get out of my sight you no good. Ahh ahh. *Bangs hands on table and throws coffee towards southern server named Eloise, but miraculously she does not get splashed.

Her: Hey send me a cute picture.

Him: You can have two. However, you can view them online under LA County's 2014 and 2015 public arrest records.

Everyone's been talking about the Olympics and talking about how they are winning gold. You're not winning gold. A group of individuals are winning. I personally am not winning anything. I'm not cashing in on Sports Illustrated royalties. I'm not staying in fancy hotels and eating gourmet meals. I ain't got no new pairs of shoes. Kids need shoes. Kids need shoes. And when I fly, I'm not flying in first class. . .. I fly in steerage, zone 3. Now how about you?

"Don't go near that guy! He's sketchy."
"How can you tell?"
"He's wearing Sketchers."

The Protagonist
"Look, its simple. I don't think you want to kill yourself on a night like tonight. I'm calling your bluff. Put the knife down!"
"I don't have anything to live for."
"Life itself is worth living for, isn't it?"
"No."
"Put the weapon down and go home. Look at this as a get out of jail free card. I don't need you wasting my time and I don't need to waste your time on Christmas Eve. Time's a valuable resource

partner. I didn't learn that in the academy. I learned that growing up on the ranch."

"Don't call me partner."

"If that knife comes any closer to your chest, I'll shoot you in the foot. You're not dying on my watch, maybe just going to the hospital. Great, there's little children watching and I guarantee they have aspirations like you once did."

"Go away cop. Maybe I'm their hero? There's always a good and a bad."

"You're not bad. You're just a scared little man boiling up inside."

"Shut up. I'm the Big Boss Man."

"Tiny man, you picked the wrong day to cross my path."

"You crossed my path."

"We crossed each other's paths."

"I'm the Baddest Dude West of the Mississippi."

"Is that so? How old are you, four?"

"Shut up!"

"Ahh I see how it is."

"I know knife-defense, self-defense, have a couple of boxing medals, and know MMA. I'm not afraid to rip that knife out of your hand faster than a snake snatching a feeder mouse."

"Bring it on."

"Don't be stupid. You're making some real bad decisions partner. Don't quit. Don't give up."

"I'll break you if you step one foot closer, then I'll kill myself."
"Oh so you're going to make a threat against an on duty officer? So you're a drama queen and a comedian? Do you want me to list your charges? My brother-in-law works for the district attorney. You want to go away for years?"
"Ahhhhhhhhhhh."
"Off the record, what's wrong?"
"She hates me."

True Story

Mr. Kim and I were in line at the gas station. I farted and didn't think much of it. A few moments later a woman nearby says "Do you realize how disgusting that is?" I froze because I got caught and was getting called out. The fart must have been silent but deadly. As I formulated an apology in my head for my stinky fart, she starts yelling at Mr. Kim for cutting his finger nails with nail clippers that were for sale near the hotdog rotating machine. He puts them back. She pressures him to grab the one he used. He gets nervous, grabs the wrong one, we leave, and the clerk shakes his head.

"You ever hear of Snap Chat? I got fired or unfollowed by Snap Chat! I was tired of receiving generic snaps like "look at me, I'm at the gym?" or snaps of food. To send a message, I filmed an action stunt. I ran to the bathroom at a community college, shut the stall door, and started recording. On film, I recorded me pulling down my pants and poop spraying out my butt. However, I missed the toilet and sprayed feces everywhere. It was the worst poop of my life. Recipients of the Snap barfed. It was a crime scene and I spent 25 minutes cleaning up my caca."

True Story

I'm not that popular of a guy, but recently got invited to a birthday party. My friend Jaun was turning 48 years old. He invited me over for chips and ceviche. After a couple of beers, I went to the bathroom to lower my BAC level and I see that he has some Q-Tips. I steal some and leave. While walking to my car, which was parked far away in Egypt, I start cleaning my ears. Now I didn't want to litter because littering is bad, but I see a kid's chocolate milk nutrient drink on a ledge. I put the used Q-Tip in the drink and keep walking, but then realize that the kid is playing around the corner and he might come and take another sip of his chocolate milk. After minutes of an ethical contemplation and fearing the worse, I went back and stole the kid's chocolate milk. I didn't want to become the main news story: *kid drinks chocolate milk with used Q-Tip; currently searching for the suspect.*

I've been working out for 7 years. On average, I go to the gym 4 days a week. That's nearly 1,456 workouts. As you can tell, the results show! In that timeframe, I have only collected 2 girl's numbers. That means I have a .00137% chance I'm going to get a girl's number. My odds of getting her to text back are 0%. Therefore, I stopped wearing deodorant when I work out.

I like to think. I like to think about thinking. Speaking hypothetically, what would you do if you were on a mid-west road with few exits and you had to poop? You drive past a sign that says "56 Miles" and you start thinking a little more. You go 20 more minutes and start calculating approximately the time of your arrival. You see another sign that says, "15 miles", but a small turd is peeking out. You squeeze, lose focus, and get side swiped. There is no damage and the other driver is clearly guilty. Would you poop your pants and handle the process after an accident with poop running down your legs and shorts and sue for emotional damage? Or do you keep driving towards the next exit that has a gas station? Meanwhile the guy who hit you is pissed off at himself and in shock because his insurance is going to rise per month. He starts hitting his hand on the arm rest because he is poor already. "Do I make a run for it or be ethical?" He moves 1 lane to the left then 1 lane to the right. Meanwhile the man in the front car is squeezing his abdominal muscles as hard as he can and is saying slowly "holy molly, holly molly, holly molly." He does not flick his turn signal to indicate to pull over. The pursuit continues.

Going furniture shopping this weekend. Should I buy the lazy boy? The love seat? The toilet or the electric chair?

The Semester

Week 1

"Balby Daun?" Silence. "Is there a Balby Daun in this classroom?" "Call me Hurley Shirt." Most of the students in Economics laughed. "Oh you guys think that's funny, huh? So we got a real wise crack in this class. Great. Just great." A guy who appeared to know Hurley Shirt gave him a down low high five. "Bethany Francis?" "Here." "Byron Mathis?" "Present." The Professor went down his roster. He took a swig of coffee and reached for unused chalk and gave it a nice sniff.

"So what do you guys know about economics?" A few students raised their hand. He panned the crowd. "Hurley Shirt, I pick you." "I didn't have my hand raised." "What do you know about economics?" "I know you got your cheap looking wool suit from the clearance rack at Ross." The students laughed. "That's two times of bantering." Sally Smith entered the tension. "Economics is what runs the currency in America and in foreign trade. It's an important part of everyone's sustainability." "Good, very good. Let me hear someone else's perspective." A chubby kid wearing a FUBU shirt in the back raised his hand.

"Yes, you in the back!" "I know that the lower per ounce price at the grocery store is the better deal. For example, A microwave chicken dinner going for 3 dollars isn't as good as a 2 for 5 dollar deal." "True very true. I personally look for those signature select pizzas to go on sale. But do you need 2 microwave dinners. The total sum is 5 dollars. That is 2 dollars more than the price for 1." The Professor lectured and wrote stuff on the board. As class was near ending, a paper ball softly hit the backboard. The Professor made a rapid scary face, one the kids could not see. His nose gently touched the chalkboard. "Who threw that?" He leaned down and picked up the wad of trash. The class looked at him with perfect attention. "Oh who made this toss? Don't try out for the basketball team. Don't ever play beer pong. Don't ever. . . .The thing is it doesn't matter. This is going to be a long long semester. The minute hand on the clock will move very very slow on my watch. The loads of homework will be pushing a fine line, a line so close that I'll be ready when the superintendent pays me a visit. The thing is, I've been doing this for some time now. I have what they call tenure. I can be a real cool guy if you guys focus, but if you start slipping it will not be fun for your GPA's. Muhahaha muhahah." The bell rang.

The seats raddled and clanked as the students vastly departed room 109. "My favorite students are the ones that snitch."

Week 2

I have now asked for you pupils to lower the volume on 4 different occasions. I have a stack of referrals with your names on it. I have the power to take away homecoming events such as the basketball game and big dance. The class lowered their voices. Then Hurley Shirt said, "I'm going to dance on the moon at the dance and touch some butt." "You're not going to the dance." The class laughed.

"Come on! I was kidding." "You don't got ears kid. You tried me and you lost." "Don't be like that!" "Case dismissed. One more word out of you and you will have a week of detention." "What's up your butt today? Is it your boyfriend?" The class started laughing. One kid wearing a blue Hanes shirt banged his head on the table and laughed hysterically. The Professor back paddled as he began to sweat. "Shut up! All of you. I'm making the test 20 problems longer and there will be no curve. This could be a fatal moment in your academic careers if you don't study hard."

That Friday The Professor decided to chaperone the dance. There were lights. Some students chose to express themselves more than others. A DJ played the album *Rituals*. Some students danced like they were dancing on the moon. Hurley Shirt stood near some bushes. In the distance, he saw The Professor talking to Ms. Fox. The two adults walked over to the fruit punch. He poured her a glass. While his back was turned, Hurley Shirt snuck into the dance, then power walked into the gymnasium. He wore glasses to hide his identity from the staff. "I grind so fine they call me coffee." Hurley Shirt boogied for hours dancing with a girl or two and some of his boyfriends on the football team. Everywhere he went, he kept his head on a swivel.

As the dance ended, students littered the parking lot hanging out on truck beds. Some cars played music while students discussed their afterschool dance shenanigans. As The Professor was leaving in his car he looked left and saw Hurley Shirt giving a girl a hug. Like a shark smelling blood, he had a strong feeling the boy had snuck in. "He won this round."

The next day Hurley Shirt hit the food court and got a popcorn and a drink combo. He made his way to the back of the store, after stopping at the toy aisle to scope the wrestling action figures. *Mossimo or Merona?* He wandered around the clothes department looking for bystanders and cameras. He walked up to a black Merona shirt and tucked it between the hand warmer of his sweatshirt and headed towards the grooming department. *Old Spice, Axe, or Body for Men?* He slipped the deodorant, a scented one the gals were sure to like, into his back pocket.

He passed a mom and daughter pushing a red cart. A guy riding an electric scooter with a blue leg cast hung out on aisle 4 browsing the dog food. *Woof.* The kid hung a left past the photo department being operated by a woman wearing khakis and a red shirt. The red revolving doors opened. "Sir come with me." A strong young adult grabbed the boy by his arm and yanked the black Merona shirt out his sweatshirt. "Let me go!" The guy tightened his grip and twisted Hurley shirt's fingers. A worker wearing khaki shorts, a red sun-beaten t-shirt, and an orange vest watched. As he was taken to Lost Prevention, The Professor happened to be checking out. The two made eye contact. The Professor made a gesture that he was number 1 and obnoxiously laughed. He then shouted "Send him to jail. Feed him to the lions."

Week 3
In class, no matter what the topic was, Hurley Shirt and The Professor took opposite sides. Every time they spoke to each other, there was tension. After a disagreement in regards to food stamps, Hurley Shirt muttered "Your face pisses me off." "Boy, I'm pretty sure you received the sperm and an egg of two bunko parents!" "I hope your credit score tanks because of credit card fraud." "That's ok, because I will always know where to find you. You will be flipping burgers your whole life." "I'd spit in your food." "I'd pop your bike tires while you're busy during a lunch rush and freaking out because you don't have an ounce of mental toughness kid." The rest of the classroom looked back and forth as the two exchanged a verbal Royal Rumble match. "Don't you pick up that phone!" Some students were scared. Others were confused. All eyes were on The Professor. He finally had the classes attention.

Week 4

A bunch of 12th Graders were passing the football around in the quad. Some made fancy catches in front of the girls watching from the lunch tables. A buff looking teen threw a high ball to Hurley Shirt. The pigskin soared through the air. Hurley shirt back pedaled then rotated his body into a small sprint. He hopped up on a cement platter. "Don't drop it" The Professor said under his breath passing by eating a ham sandwich. Hurley Shirt took his eye off the ball and got smacked in the eye. His friend's sixty feet away made painful body expressions as their classmate rolled around on the grass in pain. The Professor looked out of his peripherals as a small crowd gathered around the boy and gently fist pumped. Hurley Shirt was pissed off and boiling up inside. He couldn't understand how The Professor still had his job. He thought the man was bunko. After getting hit with the ball, he suffered a black eye for the week.

Week 6

The Professor was passing through the corridors with Ms. Fox, an English teacher. You could say she was foxy. He was acting like he was cool and

Prince Charming. "I loved your speech at the conference the other day. You certainly moved me." "Thank you. I was so nervous. Did you see how many people were there?" "There were so many people. It was amazing." All the sudden a pink eraser plunked off his forehead. His coffee slipped out of his hands, hit the ground, and splattered into the air. He dropped his stack of papers. Miss. Fox looked around trying to locate a quick suspect, but could not see a soul. His dress shoe slipped off. "Arghhhh. Ughhhhh. Muhhhhh." "Now who could have done such a thing?" she asked as she helped gather The Professor's belongings. He layed there like he had been knocked out by Tyson. In the far distance, Hurley Shirt walked towards the 300 building with his hands in the air like he was the King.

Week 8

The Professor passed back papers. As the grades started to spread throughout the class, students whispered their grades to their friends. Most received A's and B's. Hurley Shirt kept quiet. "Needs a ton of work." The word ton was emphasized with a line that zig zagged to the bottom of the page. Then there was an arrow suggesting to turn the page. To his surprise, another note. "In all my years, I've never read a worst paper. Needs to improve. I suggest you try Braille."

Week 9

Hurley Shirt got to class early and dropped a wad of bubble gum that he had been chewing onto The Professor's chair while pretending to grab a "Warm Up Exercise". It contained about six pieces of gum. During class, The Professor turned around to face the chalkboard. A long pink strand connecting from his pants to the chair stretched. The students laughed. "What's so funny?" The students looked at him. "I am scared for the future. When I get older, you shmucks will be governing this country in which I will have no power because you peoples and your ways will form the majority."

Little Caleb snitched on Hurley Shirt after he was bribed after class. "Hey Caleb can I talk to you real quick?" "What is it?" The Professor waited to speak till everyone left. "Why was the class laughing?" The behavior made no sense. "Something happened and I need you to speak up! You want 5 bucks and a candy bar?" The kid squealed. The Professor shrieked after touching the gum with his hairy fingers.

Week 10

The Professor grabbed Hurley Shirt by his backpack handles that draped over his pectorals. The hallway was empty. The tardy bell rang. "You think your tough? You think you have control over me?" He squeezed harder. The tin locker reverberated as Hurley Shirt's backpack swayed against the locks. "Let me go!" "Back in my day, the professor would challenge a naughty student to a school yard brawl on the handball courts. Meet me near the handball courts after school ya punk." The Professor let go. During 7th period both schoolyard brawlers came to a realization. *I don't want to get expelled and go to juvenile hall.* Hurley Shirt was a cop enthusiast but knew the road ahead. The Professor thought of secretly hiring Chauncey, a 200-pound princess fatty, to fight for him. Chauncey declined the offer and was slightly freaked at the proposition. That afternoon, no souls showed.

Week 11

"What are you getting for lunch?" "Pizza at the center." The Professor was angered at the inappropriate classroom disturbance of Hurley Shirt making burp and fart noises on purpose. In his swivel chair, he broke the tip of his pencil writing notes. He grabbed a pen dug and scribbled notes out of frustration. "What is this?" "One of the worst papers I've seen." "Could do this better than you at age ten." 'I can't read past line three." Another fart noise was muttered. The Professor knew nothing would quiet the boy, for nothing had worked all semester long and the school had no evidence on why the student should be removed from the class. The bell rang and the kids left the classroom in joy. The Professor grabbed his car keys from his desk and waited behind. Then he walked through the quad and past the gymnasium to the teacher's lot. He saw Hurley Shirt riding his skateboard to the shopping center. The Professor pulled behind a dumpster on the side of the pizza place then creeped up near the front window. He watched Hurley Shirt play the claw machine. The kid won no prize and his spy did a mini fist pump. His number was called and he ate his pizza in solace. After he was done eating he went to the bathroom to empty the 4 sodas that he drank. The Professor finally entered the pizza place and headed towards the bathroom. He saw kids he recognized, students from previous years. He smiled mischievously and nodded to their existence. The professional scholar waited right outside the men's restroom. Hurley Shirt took his time. The door opened and Hurley Shirt was flipped 180 degrees, back against the wall. His neck pierced into the plastic part of thumb tacks that held newspaper clippings to a bulletin board. "Who do you think you are you no good weasel punk? I swear if I was your age, I'd give you a black eye. Maybe two. You think you can misbehave and run your mouth because you're a big bad Senior? Consider this a free life tutorial." Hurley Shirt tried to push him back but the professor had his hands locked between the kid's pectorals and armpits, and one of his legs pressed against the wall facing his back. "You better cut the crap if you know what's good for you." The teacher flung him forward as he scooted out of the way. The Professor smacked the wall as he departed. Sports newspaper clippings fluttered onto the ground.

Week 12
Hurley Shirt knew that the professor drove a PT Cruiser. His license plate read "D0gguy9". Hurley shirt had some orange window paint and walked up to the car. In big letters, he wrote "BARK FAG". He looked around to make sure nobody saw him and he left. Around 4pm, The Professor walked up to his car carrying a bunch of papers. He stopped in disbelief. *The boy shall fail his Final no matter what!*

Last Day of School
Hurley Shirt stayed up till 4am studying for the final. He started at midnight after playing video games all evening. It was a Thursday morning. The test came. He finished quickly and left with confidence. In the quad, Hurley Shirt signed yearbooks and wrote HAGS. He even got a phone number from Betsy. The Professor posted the grades on the windows at the end of the day as the sun started to go down. The moment was here. Will he pass high school and go to community college next semester? To his surprise, Hurley Shirt got a D plus. He was livid. It was impossible. The system was rigged. He tried to

open the door. It was locked. He could see The Professor at his desk. Hurley Shirt made his way around to the other side of the building. He walked through a computer lab that shared a door with room 109. He barged into the room. The Professor looked up. It was like a western stare down. "You screwed me. Without a C I don't graduate." "Sucks to suck." Hurley Shirt pressed forward. "Let me do extra credit." The Professor got up. "I'll see you next semester. I hope you do a lot of growing and a lot of maturing this summer. Hurley Shirt walked over to the fire alarm. He pulled the lever. Black ink sprayed him and it started to rain unexpectedly. Hurley shirt grabbed a desk and threw it with all his might at The Professor. The heel of the desk clipped the utmost hated man in the jaw. Hurley Shirt stood over The Professor. "I win!"

Super Bowl Speech

I'm not going to lecture you on what we're doing wrong. I'm not going to break you out into your respected positions. We all know what we need to do. Many of you have been playing this game for at least 12 years. Tonight, you are fiddling with genius perfection. The glass has been shattered like a complex spider web. Will we break the glass? Will we break through? A master doesn't need to be told what to do because he problem solves. The test is 30 minutes. We will be judged. On the contrary, it's how we perceive ourselves in the light of the world. We are losing, but you are all competitors. This ain't your first rodeo!

How many times did you want to quit throughout your football careers? You didn't quit when you were living for the Friday night lights! You didn't quit when broken collarbones and bruised ribs sidelined you from playing College Game Day. And you didn't quit after getting embarrassed on national television during week 2 on Sunday Night Football. Many of you have trained in the brutalist of heat storms in the south-east through years of double days. A few of you lost family members the week of big games. Back in October, our star wide-receiver Balby Dawn had to leave the team immediately for doping. We have all faced many setbacks, but we can't let any more setbacks hold us back from achieving the long-term goal that has been instilled into our minds since we first picked up the pig skin. Every short-term goal that has been thrown your way, you all have achieved. Tonight, on the night of nights, you can capture your long-term goal. Hammy Duke, Charlie Nuegett, Adeldo Chavez, and myself all have rings. We've felt that rush of blood that pours through the veins when touching the Lombardi Trophy for the first time, but hell with it. I want to hoist the trophy with each and every one of you. Can we forget the fact that we're down by 17 points and have 83 yards for loss due to penalties? If you can find a way to be the meanest and smartest best you for the next 30 minutes, then together we will be victorious.

If you get knocked down hard, muster up the courage to say "I want some more" as you get up. If you go to the ground with one of those ugly white uniforms, let them know you will be back for more. Let them know that they are your babies. Goo-goo-ga-ga. If you think it's been a dog fight so far, let's turn this into a prison blood bath. But you guys are on the opposite side of the law.

I wish I could throw on some pads, bite my mouth piece like a dog chewing a chew toy, and step on the field, but I'm an old timer. If I got hit I bet my cleats and socks would fly off. The reason you are part of this organization is because management and myself thought you were best people for the job. Cut day is probably the hardest day of the year. It isn't easy to shatter a grown man's dreams and watch it in their face as you release them from the organization. The job is not quite yet done. Let's finish this game on our terms and shock the world. Vegas has us at 7 to 1 odds. Let's lose people some money and crush the dreams of others. One team can only be defeated and that sure as hell ain't going to be us. Not tonight. To say I'm not a nervous wreck would be a ticket to Hell for committing a terrible lie. I feel like I can't breathe. When the clock hits zero and this game is over, I want to let out an exhale like no other. One of happiness and alpha pride, not remorse. I don't want to see those tears of sadness in your eyes as you walk back into the locker room tunnel with a heavy broken heart. This opportunity may not come again. You are living your childhood dream tonight so let's capture the moment with a victory? When the night is over we don't want to think about what we could have done differently. Let's work tonight so we don't have to work again.

Think of all the people to ever play this game, but never got far. Maybe they played a few years then decided the sport was not for them. Maybe they had All Pro written over their highlight wheels, but tragedy struck. Anyone who has ever played the game has wanted to be playing in this game. Go out there and play your game. Let's dance on the moon tonight.

Graduation Speech

Hold your applause. I haven't said anything. Well I haven't said anything tonight. As I look into this crowd I see a lot of faces that I have interacted with over the last four years. I know some of your names. . .. for good and bad reasons. You all look a bit different on this day. There's a particular glow in your faces. All your life you've been influenced. Your parents, teachers, mentors, and your current beliefs have played the biggest factors in most of your past decisions. Think of it as the Lysol of influence-they have sprayed your brain with 99.99% effectiveness. But lucky you! This happens to be the 00.01%. So, turn up the volume of our own voice in your head while you are hearing this. Start today. If you can't hear your voice loud and clear, then you aren't doing it right. In the upcoming years, you will have to make huge decisions. Now here's where things get interesting. You've learned a fraction, a fraction of a fraction, a fraction of a fraction of a fraction about how this world will kick in the gut. It's how the system is designed. You might think you know all the answers because you're graduating high school and some guy on the internet said he could teach you how to make a million dollars while you sleep. Tread lightly, be cautious, be aware. One day you will be a young adult with all the answers because you've traveled a little, you've received a promotion, you've purchased a nice car on credit, and lived through a couple of great moments. You will go to bed happy on a Tuesday night thinking "life is great and I can't wait for my annual vacation." But you will wake up the next morning, go through your morning steps like brushing your teeth, only to learn minutes later that your life will never be the same. You'll go from having an assortment of options of food in the refrigerator to making a large cheese pizza last 3 days if you don't stay on top of your game. Depression will occur, most definitely. You may want to give up, but I encourage you to not. To get back to your winning self, maybe it requires you to start reading more. Maybe your new path to success means waking up at 4 am. Maybe it's taking life a little slower to be more patient to think better. There's ways to recover all that you may lose, except for family. Keep everything negative in the past and keep moving forward.

You might go from being an annoyed boyfriend or girlfriend because your love did something that may have ticked you off but wasn't that big of a deal, to a lonely person checking your phone every few minutes hoping your ex will text or call you. You might even go through a phase where you think your phone is broken because you got no calls or texts coming in for days on days. When you take your phone to the store, the clerk will laugh and pat you on the back for trying.

Every problem has a solution if the seeker seeks the answer. Thoughts will flood your consciousness and it will be critical that you take action on the thoughts that can get you to your short and long term goals. Life my friends, I can call you friends now, is an ongoing equation. It will take work. Unless you want to be someone who does not want to be industrious to society and live in the shadows of their family's wealth. The thing is I've met a great number of people over the years. They all shared one thing. They all loved to find solutions when caught in a giant hiccup.

You will meet a lot of people. There will be people you meet that will act like friends, then stab you in the back. You might even end up being the friend that stabs another in the back. If you do you may lose sleep; you will be creeping while you're sleeping. There might be a clique your trying to befriend. Six months later you'll be saying "These are my friends for life." You'll network and have a grand old time. Then a year later you'll be walking your dog on a starry night thinking to yourself "Why did I waste my time trying to impress people that didn't care about me." Basically, what I'm trying to say is that in life friends come and go, but at least their fun while they last. I spent many Halloweens' alone and was born on the 4th of July. The good thing is that you realized you needed to make change. You start thinking about how you can achieve your 10-year plan in the next 6 months. What do you want and how are you going to get what you want?

All of you will achieve greatness and there's a slim chance that you may become celebrities. On the contrary, you have the right to your own definition. In the beginning an activity is foreign to us. What is it? Never seen it before! We experiment a little keeping our eyes out for positive and negative associations. Eventually the positives will outweigh the negatives and you'll really start to like your productivity. You'll like it so much that it will become your passion. Kids once you locate passion you can achieve greatness. Just remember you sometimes must be patient while on your path to your goals. You don't need to make millions of people happy. You just have to change one person's life for the better. You can be like me, drive a Honda and be a Principal.

If you're a musician and your pissed off because no gig will sign you, but you can make a couple patrons tell you that they enjoy your music while you perform the saxophone on a busy bar street on a Saturday night in Charleston South Carolina, you win.

If you're an author not on the New York Times Best Seller List, but were told by over 200 people good things about your story, you win. When you are the one who decides what winning looks like, you win. If you let others decide what winning looks like for you, you come back and think about the speech your principal gave you on graduation day.

The End

Thank you for reading. I understand most of those jokes were a tragedy and needed a moment of silence. To keep up with my ongoing comedy career please visit my YouTube channel. Type in "Michael Alcaraz Food Pours". Food Pours is a show where I pick a random food item and pour it on my head. I've poured pizza, spaghetti, cereal, beer, etc. What will be next? Fill free to submit an idea.

If you enjoyed this book, check out my first book. It's a lot more serious in tone and a great story about a homeless teenager, turned savage, turned amateur boxer. It's currently a screenplay. You can check out *A Hollow Fight* on Amazon or iBooks.

You've added laughter to your life by reading this book. Laughter is healthy and burns calories. However, do you want to get super healthy? Check out this nutrition store in a bottle called Zeal. It targets the 5 root causes for poor health: poor nutrition, free radicals, stress, poor emotional health, and physical inactivity. Zeal is cheaper than a cup of coffee a day and changing lives. Visit zurvita.com/malcaraz1

Lastly, fill free to drop me a message at my website: michaelalcaraz.wordpress.com

www.ingramcontent.com/pod-product-compliance
Lightning Source LLC
Chambersburg PA
CBHW061256040426
42444CB00010B/2395